T0149235

What was the most terrifying nightmare you remember?

A never ending torment

Run away

You can try,
But your legs are weary

Fly away,
But your wings have been burnt

A never ending torment bestows your mind

Leaving you no other option

Then to kneel to your oppressor

And surrender to its power.

The power of depression.

Hello Friend.
Welcome.

Inside

My

Ugly

MIND

BY

JACOB GALLEGOS

Inside
my
ugly
Mind

JACOB GALLEGOS

INSIDE MY UGLY MIND

iUniverse books may be ordered through booksellers or by contacting:

iUniverse
1663 Liberty Drive
Bloomington, IN 47403
www.iuniverse.com
844-349-9409

Because of the dynamic nature of the Internet, any web addresses or links contained in this book may have changed since publication and may no longer be valid. The views expressed in this work are solely those of the author and do not necessarily reflect the views of the publisher, and the publisher hereby disclaims any responsibility for them.

Any people depicted in stock imagery provided by Getty Images are models, and such images are being used for illustrative purposes only. Certain stock imagery © Getty Images.

ISBN: 978-1-5320-7475-2 (sc)
ISBN: 978-1-6632-3323-3 (hc)
ISBN: 978-1-5320-7476-9 (e)

Library of Congress Control Number: 2019906150

Print information available on the last page.

iUniverse rev. date: 12/16/2021

Contents

AXON:

A disappearing winter 2
A familiar darkness 4
A never ending torment 6
Antidote 8
Anxiety 10
Beast 12
Beautiful and pink 14
Black Wings 16
Blood Pumping 18
Buried 20
Cage... 22
Cherry Tree 24
Cigarette 26
Clever squirrel 28
Dark Angel 30
Desperate Prayer 32
Distant ponds 34
Don't break my heart 36
Droplets 38
Drowning 40
Empty mirrors 42
Etched 44
For years 46
Gamble 48
Georgia's sky 50
Giants... 52
Goodbye, Friend 54
Half of me 56
Hard to find 58
Heart... 60
Heavy hands 62
House of fear... 64
I walk alone.. 66
I would, for you 68
In love with a sin 70

In tact 72
Iron butterfly 74
Jancel 76
Kite 78
Last day 80
Last lesson 82
Let me 84
Lullaby 86
Man in the mirror 88
Mental Dam 90
Mother 92
Mother's last goodbye 94
Muddy boots 96
Mute 98
My brother's name 100
My cross to carry 102
My favorite drug 104
My final price 106
My friends 108
My majesty 110
My sad clown 112
My warm sun 114
Naked and lonely 116
Not yours 118
Parts that make me 120
Planted 122
Platoon 124
Please 126
Questions from the deep 128
R train 130
Red from his head 132
Rotten Fruit 134
Session 136
Skin and tears 138
Soldiers legacy 140
Sometimes 142
Spare me 144
Spider web 146
Stay 148

Tears of my stars 150
That man 152
The desire 154
The strongest 156
The wall 158
Therapy...160
Thirsty 162
This is where we live...164
Three blind mice...166
To be..168
Toward clouds..170
Trenches and stitches..172
Urges..174
Very much alive 176
What she wants 178
What you did 180
When I was young 182
White stallion...184
Wind of fall 186
Wolf 188
Young sunflower 190
Your show 192
You were 194
Zero three hundred hours 196
Zodiac 198

Pages are a boring concept in my opinion. This is much more than a simple book, it is unique, like YOU. To use pg. at the bottom of every page would be to put it onto the same level as anything else. It would mean to make it generic and normal but normal is not what this book was meant to be. An Axon is a nerve fiber. It is a long, slender projection of a nerve cell. The function of the Axon is to transmit information to different neurons, muscles, and glands in our brain.

Just like every page communicates a memory, a feeling and an experience these are all AXONS leading the words from Inside my Ugly mind into your beautiful and precious one.

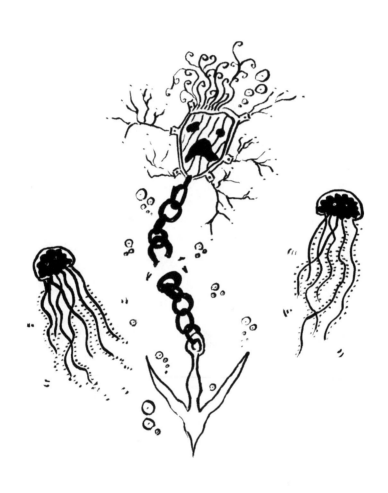

Within this book are questions.
These questions are for YOU and you only.
This is a chance to write down your answers and reasons
Of your suffering, So that you can finally begin the difficult process
Of slowly Letting go.
Pour your words of pain into this book and leave them here to die
So that you can continue to live.
J.G

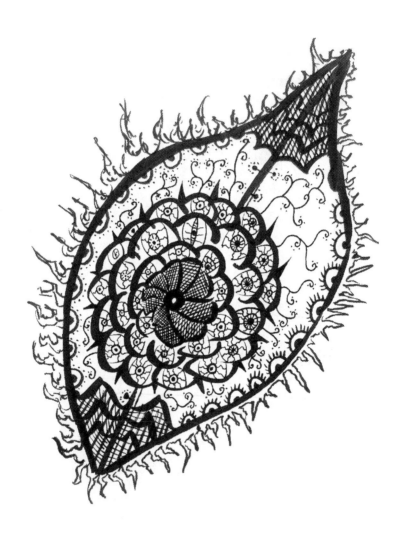

Even though I came from nothing
I still believe I am someone.
Even though I don't have nothing
I am still hungry for everything.
Even though around me there is nothing,
I still look for something.
something I've wanted my entire life
but could never touch or see.
Something that was destined for only me, which is this book
that I willingly share with YOU.

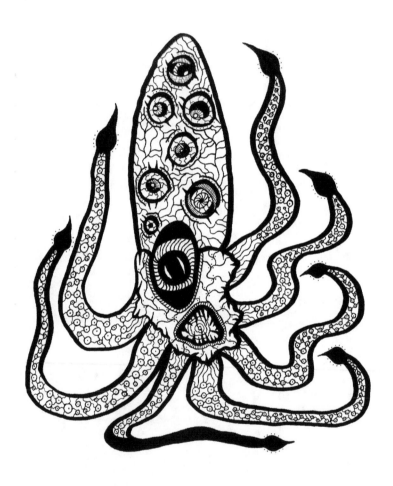

My words will contaminate you
like the saliva of a Komodo dragon.
My ideas will penetrate your mind
and poison it worse than the bite of
a King Cobra.
My thoughts will consume you faster
than a school of Piranhas.
The echo of my voice will scramble your thinking
like the screams of Cicadas
but my poetry will enchant you
like the dance of a lonely
Box Jellyfish.

Inside
my
ugly
mind

To the teachers who told me
I would become nothing
And to the teachers who
Actually taught me something.

~ Thank you all ~

Only the ink spilled from my pen
Determines the weight of my words
Like sharpened daggers
They were meant to cut deep
And like rain
They were meant to drown you
And drench you
With the wetness of my tears and blood
Not the color of my skin
Or the choice of my lust
Man or woman
They are both words
Born from ink
Buried in paper.

- Jacob Gallegos.

A disappearing winter

Drops.
Falling.
Like the heartbeat of a dying child

Drops.
Falling.
Like the bellow of a Japanese taiko

Drops.
Falling.
Like bullet casings ejected from an AR-15

Drops.
Falling.
Like the tears of a disappearing winter
Saying her last goodbye.

Which winter will you never forget?

A familiar darkness

I awaken

Lost in my own consciousness
Release me from this prison
Unleash me from its chains
Yet I know this place
I remember it

It is familiar, the darkness
I know it very well
Even better than my own damn self
Save me from its deceiving maze
From its poisonous ways

I can see something far away
Barely visible, But not so distant
There it is, my sanity
As it hangs on a fine string of Ivory

Underneath it lies my hope
Dwelling in a bottomless pit
My journey is almost over
The pain is almost gone

Fear has become my only friend
Thus the numbness begins
Black shadows cover my path
Reaching out from the blind corners of my cold dark past

They have come for me
Return me to my sleep
End my misery
Give me back my liberty

Let dusk overcome
As the colors change
My torment seems done
But I awaken once again
This torture will never end.

AXON:4

Do you remember when you were at your weakest?

Antidote

We all have Demons inside

Demons that make us want things

Whisper us ugly secrets

Demons that make us lie

Everyone has their poison

Something they need and want

Something that kills them slowly

But it's their only fucking antidote

Their only cure

To the punishment

Of having to live

With themselves.

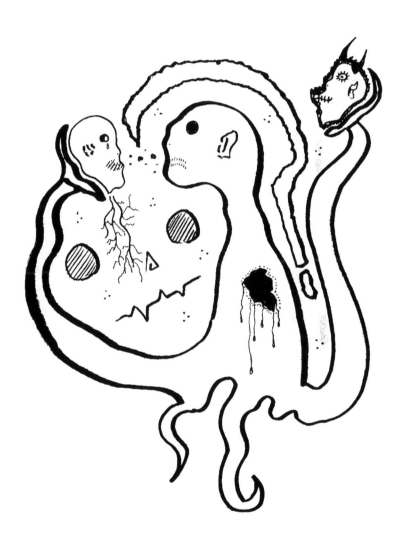

Anxiety

It is born deep within you
Where the light cannot reach
Biting and screaming
It climbs with haste
Through your sewers of guilt
And over your walls of pride
To reach the surface
Where your sanity lies
It wants to take control
Erasing all you know
Installing chaos, as you scream "no please, NO!"
And when it is done
It returns to where it came from
Low into the abyss
As it blows you an unwanted kiss
Dwelling, waiting
Until it is hungry again for the taking.

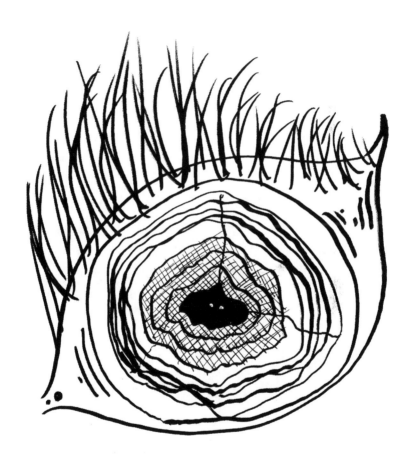

Beast

What I used to be was a reflection
A reflection of the hatred I held within
A reflection of the shadows that suffocated me
A reflection of the dreams that drowned me into depression.

Now I walk free but broken
Shattered into a hundred different pieces
Each with a thousand different reasons
And a million of different meanings
To what this life actually means

When all goes grey
When there are no more feelings for the seasons
When every breath feels like treason
And as every day my human side fails
My inner animal prevails
Growling and hissing

Scared to death and forced to the corner
Clawing at anything
Desperately fighting to survive
Bleeding more and more
As the days, slowly, go by.

My reflection is gone.
Now
I am only a beast that knows nothing but wrong.

Beautiful and pink

Your hair changes pattern
Like an octopus hugging a lantern

Your eyes are so big and full of joy
They make me want to surrender, use me I am your toy

I love your dimples, so perfectly made
Seems that god sent me an angel to love and sexually crave

Your lips are so soft, beautiful and pink
Even your other ones that drip wet like a sink

I want your tongue wrapped deep around my rock
When we are together, the last thing we look at is the time on that
damn clock.

Black Wings

My eyes fall weak
As the crow sips blood through its beak
Vision begins to fade
The final debt must be paid
Hallucinations appear
Death is near
I see its black wings
Shining, like the crown of the king of kings.

Blood Pumping

I can feel my blood pumping
Scared and frightened as if death was coming
My body viciously heats up
The water I drink is from my tears in a cup
My back aches and moans
As the subconscious in my mind suffers and groans
Anxiety and panic close in on me
Like creatures lurk in the dark of the sea
Please help me God
I feel helpless and abandoned, lonelier than a beaten dog
Do not leave me alone with myself
Please lend me a hand, all I need is your help.

When was the last time you dropped to your knees, in tears, begging for help?

Buried

My mind is my hiding place

From the monsters I must see everyday

It is my retreat

From the stupid rules of society

My withdrawal

From the fragile feelings of humanity

My shelter

From the brainwashing rain of falsity

My last dying fire

Burning to keep me safe

From the numbing cold of ignorance around me

In my mind it still snows

Buried, in my own Hell

It continues to snow.

Where do you hide to escape from society?

Cage

I have lost touch with the world

To some it may sound absurd

But my mind is like a cage

And I am trapped within it like a stolen bird

I used to be a beautiful red cardinal with a glow

Now I have been transformed into a sad and dark purple crow

I can peek through the iron bars

But life in here is so lonely, like Mars

I can see the light

But it does not see me

I can almost taste the breeze

As I still dream of one day being free

Being able to flap my wings and fly far away

But I am still locked inside this cage of solitude and grey.

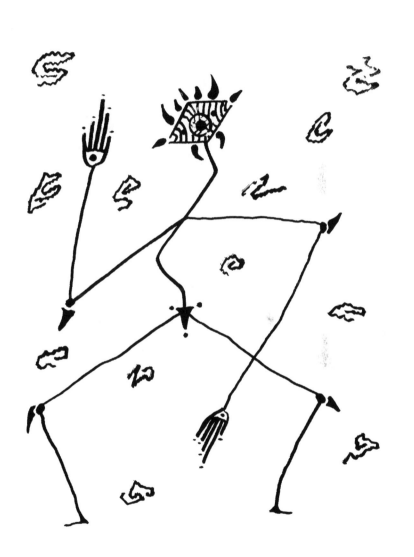

Cherry Tree

Don't bargain with love
It is an impregnable fortress
An uncontrollable wave
In a chaotic, storming ocean
You cannot buy it because it has no price
True love comes around only once in life
A gift that only God can grant
But it is up to us to take care of it
Let it grow unharmed and protected
As it blossoms beautifully
Like a cherry tree in spring...

Or foolishly destroy it
And watch it burn to the ground.

Has your love tree ever been burnt or did you start the fire?

Cigarette

It comes in a box

Sleek and elegant like a fox

Its best friend is the flame

Every time it has a different name

She loves kissing your lips

As she glows red on the tip

She wants to be inside of you forever

And when she leaves

She flies away, just like a feather.

Have you ever been addicted to a toxic lover?

Clever squirrel

Clever brown squirrel

Climbing up old father tree

Higher and higher.

No one can define what love for a friend is.
How you can be where you want to be
In this world or in this life
But if they are not with you
You feel only half complete
Only half full.
No one can understand how loving a person
Without need for sex, money or drugs is because
just their presence and company
Is more than you can desire in this universe.
To be understood and appreciated is what everyone wants.
The gift of true friendship goes beyond love and pleasure.
Their love for you is the treasure you always wanted to receive
But could never find.
That is why you will always miss your true friends.
No matter what.
No matter where.
They reserve a place in your heart
As do you, in theirs.

J.G

Dark Angel

Who goes there? Silent in the wind
Is that you, old friend?
You left so long ago
Now you come with shadows from below
Feels like an eternity
But I haven't lost my loyalty
Kiss me now dark angel
Love me, if only you are still able
Take this pain away
Please make this my last day
Hold my hand my friend
For this is my last page
My cold, dark end.

To not admire the teachings of ancient knowledge
Is to be ignorant of the very past
That gave birth to all present
and everything that will be
of the future.

J.G

Desperate Prayer

What is my purpose?
Is this life even worth it?
From how high will we fall?
How low must we descend until we lose it all?
Can you hear me from your high kingdom?
I know I am just a mortal, nothing more than a walking phantom
But if you can hear me please answer my questions
Forgive me of my errors, they were never my intentions
I know I don't talk to you much
But please reach out to me, let me feel your touch
Don't leave me here to rust
Because alone and abandoned
I will return to dust.

When was the moment you were abandoned?

Distant ponds

Distant ponds hug the cloud's dark shadows

While blue birds pierce the sky like burning red arrows

The brown spider begins spinning its invisible web

As lady sparrow and her young prepare to go to bed

Two lime green Dragonflies dance on purple water

Glow bugs shine their lights looking for their lover

As father sun falls gently asleep

Mother moon begins to awake her hungry creatures in the deep

What was the most beautiful scene you have ever seen?

Don't break my heart

CUT my chain of thoughts

BLOW my mind to dust

RIP apart my emotions

BURN my feelings alive

SHATTER my senses into pieces

But please ..

Just DON'T break my heart.

When was your heart truly broken? Did anyone ever fix it?

Droplets

Amongst the trees lies a pattern
Hidden from society
Waiting to be found
They sing to one another
Using droplets of melted ice
Drip... drop...
Making tiny holes in the snow
Every drop has a different sound
But they all share the same rhythm.

Sometimes it's hard just being.
Being tied by the pressures only you can bare.
Being lost like a compass within a magnetic field.
Being scared by a quick future
To not enjoy the current and slowly present.
Being tired and hurt like an animal
That has no more will for scars.
Being sad and confused
Like the eaglet whose mother never returned.
Just being
Is sometimes too much.

J.G

Drowning

I wish I could dive into your mind

Understand your deep waters

And the abyss

You so much hate

The part of you that keeps drowning

Crying for help

Waiting for a miracle

Waiting

For a splash of

H

O

P

E

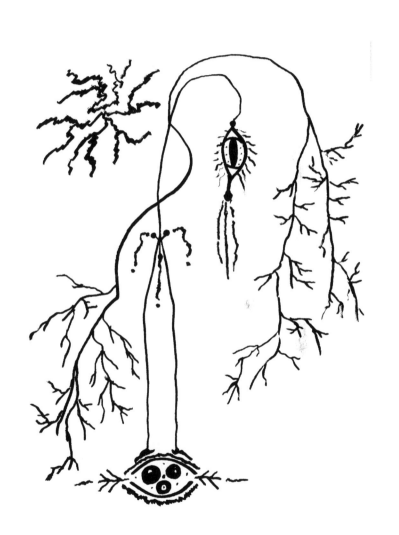

Empty mirrors

You whip me with stinging guilt
You Smack me with cold sadness
You drown me low, in my very own bloody tears
You choke me savagely with asphyxiating fear
You punch me hard with solid numbness
You cut me deep with a blade of agony
Break this fucking mirror!
And cover the rest of them
Because the man I see in the glass is my worst enemy
But without him,
the reflection in my mirrors
will forever remain empty.

Have you ever covered every mirror in your house
because you could not stand seeing yourself?

Etched

My heart won't stay quiet

It cries every night

What you did to it was fucked up

You played with it

As if it were a rubric cube

Shuffling my chambers

Towards dark dead ends

Numb with pain

It was only after you stabbed me

That I realized, I keep within me

The signature of your scar

Etched upon my fragile heart.

For years

For years I stood still,

Waiting for you to come back,

Thirsty for your rain.

We are born into the mud
Squirming to survive
Like worms
Always gazing towards heaven
Where the peaceful blue never ends
Dreaming we can soar through the clouds
Without having to hide beneath the darkness of filth.

J.G

Gamble

I don't miss the city

And I don't think the city misses me

I used to be pretty

Now I'm sad and ugly

Don't you dare look at me

I used to believe in fantasies

But reality brutally killed all my dreams

I thought it would be easy

But I guess that's the gamble of being free.

I will never be clean again
because I was born to be the instigator,
The denier
The trouble maker
The accuser
The undertaker
The cloud chaser
The wish seeker
The day breaker
The love hater
The fire starter
The wind changer
The soul taker
and
The lonely bastard
Whose only job was to be the exact opposite
of everything I ever knew.

J.G

Georgia's sky

What spectacular view

Simple and blue

Georgia's sky

Nothing but food for the eye

Like kind giants

Forming an alliance

Cotton shaped clouds

Drift slowly above

Look up

And you will see God's love.

It is better to live alone and free,
Rather than trapped within the grasps of bad company.

J.G

Giants

As children we cry

The great giants have fallen

Our heroes of time lay dormant

As they sleep like ancient ruins

Buried, under a blanket of dust

Their bellow echoes

Through our hollow clouds of greed and lust.

Who was a giant in your childhood?

Goodbye, Friend

I have seen you grow

Been with you since you were little

Saw you crawl

Helped you walk

Ran along your side

As I will

Always

Till the day I can no longer run

Till the day my last note

Will be sung.

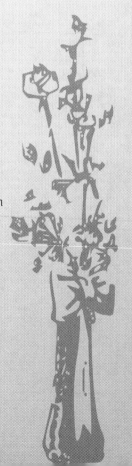

Have you ever had to bury an animal you loved so deeply?

Half of me

You only see half of me

Nothing more than you want to believe

You can't see the part that shows my ugliness

The faces of the demons inside my head

And the eyes of the stalkers

Within the walls surrounding my bed

You don't see the dark side

The fraction of my machine

That shows the gears to my beast

Fierce and untamed, like a Wolverine

You cannot target my veiled unit

Hidden within me

Concealed in the deep

Dangerous and armed, like a Russian submarine.

You will always see, only half of me.

How much of yourself do you truly hide from others?

Hard to find

Years have passed, since the last time I saw you

I still can't look at you

Even though I forgave you long ago

But I don't forget

No, no, no...

all the things you did to me

I put them in a box, see?

And I stored it away, inside my Ugly mind

So that it's hard to find

Just like you were

When I was young.

Always,

hard to find.

Who was hard to find when you were a child?

Heart

I can feel its vibration

I can feel its frequencies

I can detect its movements

I can hear its whispers

I can taste the air it breathes

I can sense its presence

I can listen to its cry

I can capture its sadness

But nothing can touch my heart.

Buried beneath the salted skin and broken bones of my
chest, Fortified by all the veils of shame, pain and regret.

Think twice before asking a question your mind seeks,
Because your heart might not be ready for the truth.

J.G

Heavy hands

Heavy hands beat the drum

As cold ones hold the gun

The gelid air burns your throat

As smoke and fire rises beneath the boat

Father knows all

What is right and what is raw

But in the end, death is the one true king

And she will, one day, have us all.

Some people do not wish to be illuminated.
They would rather live a simple happiness,
Below the light, in the shade.

J.G

House of fear

Welcome, my dear, to the house of fear

Surrounding you is the stench of death

Please do not hold your breath

Breathe it in

Let it sink

As it slowly and painfully burns your nostrils

You want to drink but around you are only empty bottles

Give up child you are my guest

Now keep your eyes closed

We'll take care of the rest.

Is there a house you never want to see again?

I walk alone

As I lay weak

Ice cold branches grow within me, deep

My shoulders feel used and beaten

Like the tracks of a railway

My mind cannot think straight

All my thoughts slither away

my knees feel fragmented, to a point that is unknown

Chiseled and broken Like aged stone

My feet are in pain

Like nails sinking in, closer and closer to the bone

Because of the weight I carry

The suffering I hold

The burden I bring

and the troubles I hide

All of these

I cannot share

With no one

Lonely as I am inside my Ugly mind

I walk alone

Searching for a place, to finally call home.

To live an honest but lonely life
Is sometimes the only way
To escape the corruption of pleasures.

J.G

I would, for you

I would slit my wrists
And let my blood pour all over you
Just to keep you warm.

I would give up food and water
And let my body decay
Just to make sure you live.

I would give you my eyes
Just so you can see
How fiercely I look at you.

I would give you my heart
Just so you can feel it
Feel how hard it beats for you.

To say I love you is not enough
It goes beyond love
My purpose of life is nothing without you

And...

I would leave you my ugly mind
But it is too much of a burden to own.

It will always be my cross
My Pandora's Box.

What was the most you gave and lost in
the dangerous game of love?

In love with a sin

I'm in love with a sin
That reflects what I need within
I see his body as armor I desperately want to wear
Trust me, I would lie if I said this life was fair
I have never seen my father
And sometimes I try not to bother
They know him as the all mighty and the one true just
But please father, forgive me, for I am a slave to this wrongful lust.

Have you ever been accused of being a monster
when you were just trying to be your true self?

In tact

Stab me in my lungs
Take my air away
Kick me in my ugly mind
Stomp it
Squash it
End the voices I hear
Rip out my spine
Disconnect me from this place
Punch me in my heart
Pound at it with ALL YOUR STRENGTH
There is no reason for it to be
End my suffering
This misery that keeps buffering
But leave my soul in tact
I wish to live again
I know that for a fact.

I am no longer me,
If I must be like you.

J.G

Iron butterfly

We are born into this world crying
Screaming, gasping and kicking

We have been removed from the safest of places
From our mother's womb
The soft warm inner shell in which we are formed

And as a bright light blinds our sight
There is nothing that can take us away from our fright

That is, until she holds you

In that moment she is the only thing that makes sense
Amazing, how a few seconds can be so intense
No amount of blood or tears can change her love as a substance

And as we grow we learn that life is unjust and hard
It's a struggle, a hustle and sometimes a chaotic rustle

We all are like butterflies at a certain point
Vulnerable, weak and harmless
But also gentle, graceful and beautiful

Then troubles come and we are cast into
A life of pain that covers us like melted iron

And if we survive, the cast will dry

But we can no longer soar high
For an iron butterfly will never fly.

I took this picture in Italy when I was young. This picture always made me feel a certain way so I wanted to share it with you. I don't know why but I've always been more attracted to moths rather than butterflies. Perhaps it's their hidden beauty that only few can see and appreciate.

Jancel

She sits on her chair

Like a cat watching the sunrise

She is tired and weak

Lost and frightened

Yet she still gazes onto the horizon

Her eyes say everything

Her pain, her battles and her war

She will find happiness one day

But not today

Have peace child

She then slowly drifts away.

Whose eyes will you never forget?

Kite

Demon, oh demon, on the wall
Why did you pick me out of them all?
Every day feels like the beginning of fall
Numbing cold,
never ending fog and scattering winds,
blocking my call
I dwell in the shadows of the trees, oh so tall
My emotions bounce around, just like a ball
Anxious and terrified I run through this dark and scary hall
I am no more than a puppet, a simple broken and torn up doll
Let me be, just for this night
Uncover my eyes, so that I can see the light
Cut these strings, I promise I won't fight
Please let me sleep
So that I can dance amongst the clouds
And let go of the pain I keep
Let me soar in my dreams
Everything is so much more than it seems
Untouched and so kind
Let me fly away peacefully, like a kite.

When I cry, I die.
But when I laugh, I live.

J.G

Last day

If God appeared to you and said today is your last day

Would you run away?

Or would you stay?

And if you stay then what will you do, what will you say?

And what of your son and daughter, your baby?

Would it be easy?

Some might say maybe

And what of your brother and sister?

Do you still love him?

Do you still miss her?

Your mother awaits you on the other side

She was given to you God, like a beautiful young bride

I never met my father

Now it's too late I'd rather not even bother

But what of your love

Your soulmate, your dove?

The only one you love

The only one you care for

Will you abandon them?

Or will you follow the light through the glass door?

What would you say to them?

If today was your last day?

Do you live with words you were never able to tell someone you loved?

Last lesson

We were supposed to be together

You promised forever

Do you even remember?

I thought you loved me and my ugly mind

Instead, you lied and left me behind

I've spent days of my past

And years of my life on you

Minutes murdered on my watch

Hours hogged from my time

Seconds sunk into a lost cause

All for you

The last lesson

I no longer want to learn.

When was your last lesson you had to learn the hard way?

Let me

Pick me up

Throw me high

Let me go, let me fly

Don't call my name

I am no longer him

Close my eyes

Let me die.

The dark part of my mind is a room I must keep locked because it contains an evil that I cannot correct.

J.G

Lullaby

Lulla, lulla, lullaby

Oh, so sweet

Caress me like a baby

Put me gently to sleep

Kiss me good night

Defend me from my terrors

Ascend me into flight

Break these false mirrors

And forgive me of my dark errors.

Depression is the rotting of the mind
And the mold that covers our heart,
Slowly eating away.
Until there is nothing left to consume.

J.G

Man in the mirror

I woke up one night
It was dark as fuck
So I switched on the light
There he was, just my luck
It was the man in the mirror
Powerful and handsome
He looked straight into me
With curiosity and envy
As he stared maniacally at my soul
It felt intense
Like falling down an endless hole
As he stood there, shirtless and all
I just couldn't stop looking at him in awe
But before I could speak
His face expression turned deep
And as I said: "I love you"
He replied:
"I think I love you too."

I would rather dive into the deepest part of the ocean
Than descend into the darkest part of my mind.

J.G

Mental Dam

Every time you said you hated me,
I cried.
Every time you regretted me,
I cried.
Every time you used me,
I cried.
When you told me that I will burn in hell,
I cried.
But every tear I shed
Is a drop,
Kept still in my mental dam
Waiting to burst open
And release against you
The anger
Of my motherless waterfall.

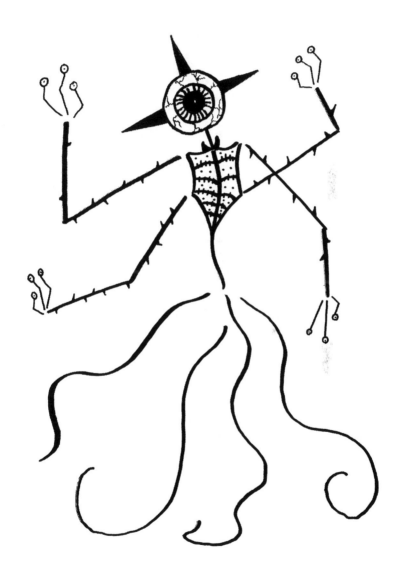

Mother

Can you remember
The love of your true mother?
Because I cannot

Mother's last goodbye

Sleep, my son

Your day has been long

Your struggle is sincere

Close your eyes

And picture the sky

Now transform for this night

And begin your flight

Soar, my son

As the proud eagle you have become.

Even though you are alone,
Your life is still an interesting show.

J.G

Muddy boots

I slowly sink my boots into the mud
My ugly mind full of thoughts, begins to overflood
Color begins to fade
As the days become old and grey
My body grows weak
Sometimes I forget how to speak
When will this struggle end?
My will is not broken but it is slowly starting to bend.

I am not your towel to dry your fear upon.
I am not your trash to dispose of your lies.
I am not your sponge to clean up your mess.
I am not your punching bag to release your anger upon.
I am no longer something to use
But I am still someone you will always need.

J.G

Mute

Can you speak, stranger?
What have they done with your tongue?
Mute, like trees in snow.

Were you ever silenced from expressing yourself?

My brother's name

As the sun starts to awake

Water drips from the last snowflakes

Red and green and all sorts of colors

Similar they stand like a picture of loving brothers

They grew up together

And now man wants to separate them forever

As their branches touch

One brother says to the other

"I will miss you so much"

Suddenly the iron beasts begin their dirty deeds

Tearing , ripping , cutting my brother trees

After the slaughter comes a new Dawn

All left is their stumps , the rest is all gone

This murder was cruel, unjust , viscous and wrong

I can still feel him as our roots are coiled in a bond

From now on This place will never be the same

Only the leaves will continue to whisper my dead brother's name.

My cross to carry

I know you did not ask to be born with this
A gift for you
A burden for me
Everyone has their own cross to carry
You may think yours is heavy
Until your neighbor gives you theirs
That is when you'll want yours back
Because you know its weight
It has been with you your whole life
And maybe one day
You'll be able to ask
Why was I given this cross to carry?
Maybe one day you will be grateful
Because carrying it
Made you stronger, wiser
And even though it gave you all your scars
It defines who you truly are.

It was in the woods
Where I would run free.
It was in the woods
where I chose my favorite tree
Because it was strong and sturdy
Friendly and safe
Old and wise,
Like my father was to me.

J.G

My favorite drug

I wish to lose myself in your smoke
Life sometimes feels like a big bad joke
Raise me high, Love me deep
Make me happy you are my weed.

Please stay still, let me sniff you
Enter my body, there is no issue
Take away this pain
As if you were my cocaine.

Pour your love into me
And let me dance with you all night
Don't let go, keep me standing tall
Please be my alcohol.

Let me swallow you, my love
Beautiful, round and bright like the moon
Trap my body in your sweet net
You will always be my Percocet.

You have always been my favorite drug
But for now, all I need, is your strongest hug.

Is there a hug you will never forget?

My final price

You tell me I am the only one

You beg me not to go numb

Have you forgotten our deal?

Sometimes none of this feels real

I am done playing your game

No matter what, I can still hear their names

You kept me a prisoner for far too long

Everything around me is false and wrong

Speak to me my friend

Will you be there in the end?

In this place the fire is as cold as ice

And in this place, I will pay my final price.

Sometimes the future is not worth spoiling.
Asking about tomorrow always ruins my today.
I'd rather replay the good times that I've lived and laughed
so that I can remember
How happy I was,
When I was young and didn't care.

J.G

My friends

Many friends come see me at night
Not sure if everything in my head is all right
She is the first
But definitely not the worst
I don't know her name
She always looks the same
Her face is rough, distorted and full of cuts
She runs after me at night only to disappear into dust

The second, is the trench coat man
He simply does not give a damn
His coat covers him from head to toe
Rather than a friend, he is more of a foe
He follows me around and stalks my life
It's like feeling hateful eyes, hiding a knife

The third one is special
First time I saw her, my fear was interstitial
She comes to me through water
Sometimes I just wish she wouldn't bother
As the drops rain over my head, my eyes start to close
And there she is, screaming at me, frozen in her same pose
Her face gushes and drips with blood
Seeping from her empty orbits as dark as mud
She dresses as the Virgin Mary
But represents a whole different type of scary
I can go on all day talking about how deep her hatred is
But maybe all she wants is a warm hug and a kiss

The last one
Fears none
It walks like a human
And is everything except one
His true nature is that of an animal
A giant sloth whose appetite is that of a cannibal
He stands in the dark, near your bed, quiet and tall
Looking down at you with an eerie silence, like a creepy tree in fall
His eyes are like a shark's, black and full of death
And when it speaks, your ears go deaf
It does not blink
His stare is so loud, it won't let you think
He has sharp claws that dangle long
Muddy and dirty, scratching the wall, he plays his song
A lullaby of fear
A lullaby that only I can hear.

My majesty

Die my majesty
Abandon yourself to death
So that I can revive you inside my ugly mind
As you soar high
And conquer all fears, all troubles and sorrows
Free me of all my doubts
Release me of my duty
This burden of life.

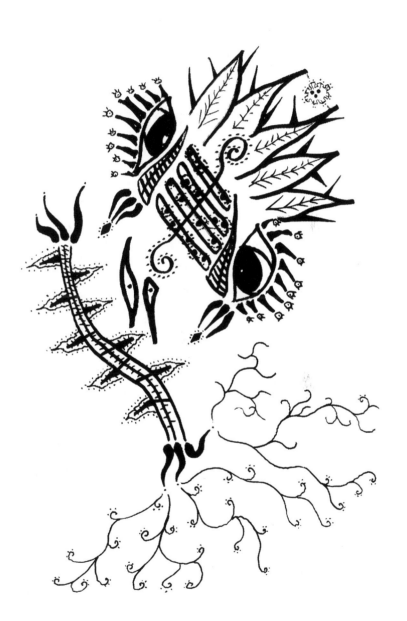

My sad clown

He laughs
While he cries
He always does
He comes to me when I am at my worst
One of my different friends
Born inside my ugly mind
Raised in my subconscious
He is crazy and I don't like him
But he is a part of me
My sad clown.

My warm sun

You used to be warm

And glowed like the sun

But ever since the day you left

All we had, went numb

All we held, fell cold

All we loved, slowly froze

Leaving me alone in the snow

Waiting for my warm sun

To come back home.

AXON:114

Alone, I cried to the wolves
Hoping someone would cry with me.
Alone, I shouted at God
Waiting for an answer
Or a sign.
Alone, I walked
Through the dark forest
Inside my mind
Still searching for a path.
A path
To lesser tears
And more signs.

J.G

Naked and lonely

Do not look at me
I am naked and lonely
But please don't leave me

We aren't afraid of what we can see
but of what we feel is watching us
like silent eyes in the midst.

J.G

Not yours

You dress yourselves in vanity
But truth is, you don't give a fuck about humanity
You Claim your pride and show your riches
The skin on your skin is not yours
The teeth in your mouth are not yours
Your face is the opposite of what truly lies beneath
You sold your heart as well
Nothing seems to be too cheap
It's easy hiding behind all the jewelry
Bright and shiny, distracts them from seeing your tears
You tore pieces of yourself off
And you paid dirty money for it
How can you remember your home, child
If you tore down everything you ever knew?

Do you even still feel pain?
Wearing a skin that is not yours
I guess not.

Parts that make me

I cannot remember the last time I saw my sanity

Year after year

I've changed more than a shapeshifter

Travelled more than a nomad

Lost parts of myself

Like a sunken ship

Pieces of me

Broken and fallen into the deep

Reflections and feelings of past memories

Parts to my puzzle that I can no longer reach

Parts that make me

ME.

Planted

No matter how hard it howls
Don't let the wind rip you away
You may lose your leaves
Your branches might snap
But your roots will always remain planted
Woven into the flesh of loving Mother Earth.

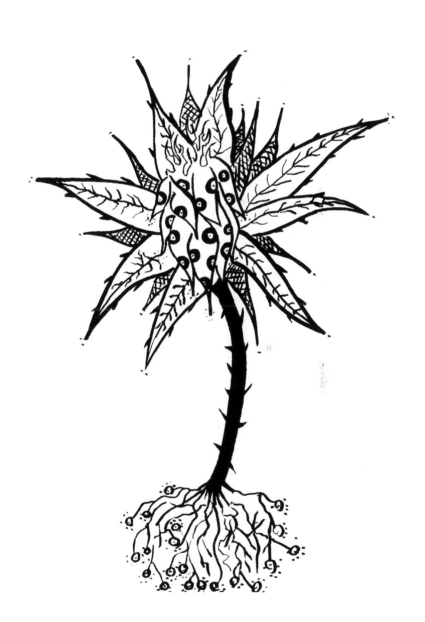

Platoon

They dress in the same manner

With different types of pattern

A color similar to green

The same that mother nature gleams

They can yell, stomp and shout

Together they will fight

There is no doubt.

Do not mistake my femininity
For weakness,
Or my openly powerful love
For kindness.

J.G

Please

Can you remember me?
I am the child within you
The one who has always loved you
You were my best friend
How come you never came to see me again?
What happened to you?
You are different
Are you no longer my friend?
Do you still love me?
I cannot finish this puzzle YOU left behind
Please don't forget me
Come and play with me
You are my only friend
Please...
Don't leave
I want to see the light that you promised me
Please,
My only one true friend.

Everyone has an inner child that cries for them
at night. What does yours cry for?

Questions from the deep

Why is it that I am what I am?

Is there a reason To be forsaken?

I am only a lonely mortal

How much should I struggle

For the only dream I seek?

How hard will the wind hit me?

How many times

Shall I have to get back up on my feet?

What my ugly mind won't let me keep

Are these questions from the deep.

What are your deep questions?

R train

Faceless emotions

Everyone sits quiet

All are tired and weary after a long day

Metal grinds upon rusty steel

Screeching, hissing, aching

The ride sways left, right

Up and down

Like a boat sailing the sea

The slow humps and turns

Put most to sleep

We travel below the ground

On rails covered in grime and filth

Hidden from the late-night lights above

But it doesn't bother them

4 more stops to Brooklyn.

Your breath smells like your sex life.
Disgusting
And pointless.

J.G

Red from his head

"I need the time"
"The clock is broke inside my mind"!

"I need time"
"I still question which thoughts are truly mine"

"But there are none"
He said, as he looked straight down into the barrel of his gun

You can't give it
You can't take it

And as the flames cornered his room
The smoke swept away his doubts, like a broom

He closed his eyes and gently squeezed the trigger
Waiting for that one bullet left his mouth dry and bitter

CLACK...
CLACK...
PAAAAAAK...

As he fell backwards onto his bed
On the wall were pieces of his mind, red from his head

Dripping down slowly, like tentacles in the dark
He never realized this was his last work of art

Burning clocks, Will never freeze time
Inside an ugly mind.

Somehow,
Someway.
Chaos
Always knows
Where to find us.

J.G

Rotten Fruit

I was born out of pity
Delivered with toxicity
Mother taught me hatred
Too many nights, crying in bed

Father taught me to survive
To forget my past
To live
To thrive

Sadness used to follow me
Wouldn't let me dream
Depression made me numb
My heroes are all gone
Solitude defined me
Born a rotten fruit
From a disturbed tree
My path has been rough
But you, out of all
Taught me love.

Everyone wants their cake
but no one wants to pay.
Our system is flawed,
We reward the odd
And we have begun to forget God
Because of the lies stirred
Into the minds of our young.
Lost
In the fog of a school system that is wrong.

J.G

Session

Take a deep breath
"Focus", she says

"Let's begin, close your eyes and breathe"
My lungs slowly expand, than retract
I can feel the cold air pulling me back

The light begins to fade
I swiftly detach myself from this world
Only to be welcomed into my subconscious.

As a weak light slowly emerges
A door stands in front of me
It seems to have always been there
It has no knob, no handle, nor a hole for a key
It is not I who chooses when it opens but rather something from within

I hear a voice as it moans in pain
Then another and another
Again and again

They all sound the same.
They all know my name.
They all patiently waited in silence with shame.

The door suddenly opens leading towards a steep passage
There are no other floors, only one stop
Low below in the bottom covered by fog.
I choose to enter the darkness.

As I descend they call out for me
Some love me
Others hate me

I can see where they lurk
In small cells around a spiraling downward fall
This place is a prison
Where all are forgotten and their names will never be heard of again.

AXON:136

The bottom is near
The voices disappear

The air stops

As the walls slowly open
Like the mouth of a dying Gargoyle
A dungeon path leads straight to one room
Defended by a fortified door
There is an eerie silence
Something behind the door laughs
It knows I am here.

From a small shallow opening and With a deep crackling tone, it says:
"Its been years since we last met"
This thing knew me better than the rest
And in my hand was the key to the caged beast
Whose name I promised never to spit again.

To open would mean to release an evil I have buried so long ago
To keep closed would mean to never be able to feel the power
and the warmth of the flames that kept me alive for so long.
The beast than speaks:
"I will always be the greatest and darkest part of you, whom
without, you will forever be incomplete."
"Isn't that why you are here?"

Damned to do, Damned not to.

In the end, He was right.

Skin and tears

I miss running in the rain

Letting it wash me clean

From the pain of a confused home

From the anger of solitude

And from the grips of fear

As I played in the mud

On the skin and tears

Of my loving Mother Earth.

Soldiers legacy

Silent we stand

As still as winter trees

Beneath the snow

Under the rain

Working swiftly like bees

Lifeless are our eyes

Emotionless and sleep deprived

Tonight, we lay guard

We seek no reward

No thankyous

No goodbyes

All has been said

We shall see them once again

Forever, until the end.

My eyes are not mine.
They were given to me
By the ghosts of my past.
I used to be blind
But now,
I can see everything.
The sadness
The pain
The misery
Of all,
While everyone else
Still walks this earth
Blind to everything
Because of the lies of few.

J.G

Sometimes

Sometimes I dream of sleeping on a cloud
Able to spread my wings and fly happily and proud

Sometimes I feel like running away as fast as a rabbit
After all these years, this cross I carry has become a habit

Sometimes I reflect on life,
Losing myself inside
My own damn ugly mind
When the truth is, no matter what, all bad things should be left behind

Sometimes my heart cries at night
Because it misses you too fucking much
I would sell my soul just to let our bodies touch

Sometimes I love you so deeply
My hunger for your body is so fucking needy
You are my food, my fuel and the reason why I am so greedy

Sometimes I become so damn thirsty for your juicy wet lips
Not only the ones with which you kiss...

What do YOU feel sometimes?

Spare me

Day after day
My nightmare is the same
My struggle prolongs
It never ends
I plead for mercy
But it has no heart
Nor soul
Only hunger for my hope
For the light within me
Whatever little is left
I beg you
Spare me
Please let me rest.

How will children care for our land
If we do not teach love For mother nature?
How will they respect one another
When we reward rudeness and inflate their heads with anger?
How will children learn from their errors
If we pamper, spoil and justify?
The old ways taught humbleness
But the new ways teach greediness.
All is yours!
Take everything!
But what have you truly done to deserve what you claim?

J.G

Spider web

Be the spider, Copy its way
And knit your mind gently like a web

Art was meant to show what the eyes could not see
And what words could not describe.

J.G

Stay

Cover me with your love
Wrap me inside of it, as tight as a glove
Sing to me with your gentle voice
Caress me while I fall asleep
Protect me from my nightmares
You're the only one I have, no one else cares
Stay by my side
Please do not hide
Stay with me tonight
Please don't leave my sight.

Tears of my stars

I have been hiding from the light

Trying to remain quiet

Isolating myself in the long night

Anchoring myself to my temporary grave

Attempting to remain safe

Camouflaged in the shade

Tired but not alone

Because the tears of my stars

Will always continue to glow.

That man

Make me your husband
Make me the man you want to love
The one that makes you feel like a dove
The man who always gives it you rough
The man that awakes you with kisses
The one that will take you to places
The man who puts you to sleep
With sweet and passionate, slow sex
The one that is so mysterious and sensual
He will leave you complex
The man that will be the father to your children
The one who will always take care of you
And won't trade you
Not even for a million
Because you will always be one in a billion.
Let me be that man.

The desire

I want you
I desire you
If I could eat you, I would
Sometimes I won't speak, even though I should
Only because our bodies talk
Letting our flesh lock
First, I kiss your skin
So good I want everything within
From head to toe
I won't let you go
Once my tongue reaches your slit
That's when I'll start to bite, just a bit
I can see your chest rise
As your beautiful breasts collide
Your nipples are hard
And so is my rock
As my big head reaches your soft wet lips, the bed starts to rock
Sink your claws into my back
While I grasp you with my paws and sniff you like crack
Hold onto me
Never let go
And when we are done let us lay together
As we kiss and hug, praying for the worst weather.

Have you ever awoken in sweat after dreaming of a desired lover?

The strongest

No matter what
It will haunt me forever
Till the day I drop
This never ending darkness is my shadow
It will never leave my side
So I learned to love it
Use it
And abuse it...
Even in the darkest of places
A seed can still grow
It will never be the prettiest
Nor the most precious
But it will be the strongest
No matter how low from the sky
It will survive
And continue to thrive...
Breaking through the toughest mountain
It wants to drink from God's fountain
Born in the shadows
Its pain echoes
It desires one day to fly with the crows
And to slumber in the deepest darkest of holes
And when it will be old
Its story around the world, will already have been told.

There you go again little bird
Flying away from tree to tree
Wondering why you just can't find the one to be.
You've tried the tallest
You've tried the smallest
The crooked, the curved and the broken
But for some reason you always fly back to me
Even though I've been burnt and grow only thorns
Deep down
You always know that within me
You will always have a place to call
HOME, sweet home.

J.G

The wall

There in the desert
Stood a lone wall.
How did we get to this point?
Allowing tons of cement, divide us all
No bridge
No window
No door
No point of connection, yet it grows more and more
My son loved a girl on the other side
He will never see her again
She will never be his bride
The road to salvation is cut off and blocked
Just like livestock we are stuffed, shoved, burnt and locked
This has truly left its mark
Not even the sun can change this place
For it will always remain sadly dark.

Have you ever had to put up an emotional barrier
between yourself and another person?

Therapy

Relentless, continuous noise

Vibrates out from his gross shallow mouth

Frantic gestures of schizophrenic movement

Are produced from the dance of his cold, stiff arms

Unresponsive muted laughter

Followed by Edge cut wide eyes

Seeking their attention

He tries to connect his bridge

But my fire will always burn it.

Thirsty

I asked the lord to forgive me
Forgive me for wishing you death
Death I asked for, every night
As I slept, disturbed in bed
You cannot see what I see
At night things come to me
A monster is not what I asked to be
lonely and useless
Tasteless
Like an old dying tree
Black within
From all my sins
Planted in grime and tar
So I wouldn't grow too far
I wonder if he will ever forgive me
If he even still loves me
If maybe he'll show mercy
Only God knows how long I've been thirsty.

They sent me the hospital bill
A bill for my health
With a number on it
That I don't agree with
A total that represented indignity
A number too high to even say
They want YOU to pay
For the help that they have
Pay for the water to drink
Or die stranded and dehydrated
No different than a business
Dividing me from my better self
From my healthy self
From my true and happy self.
All because I do not have the numbers they want.
They are the business
That lives on funding the dead,
Investing in the dying
And capitalizing on the living.
FUCK them and FUCK this letter!
Now I know what I'll use for my toilet paper.

J.G

This is where we live

Around me fly empty bags
Like ghosts haunting the streets
Gum stuck to the cement
Like leeches on warm meat
Plastic spoons and forks are scattered
Like broken pieces of wood after a hurricane
Cigarette butts are dropped and forgotten
Like rusty pennies in an ocean
Food is thrown and left to be picked at by pigeons and rats
While a baby dies from hunger across the world
And even though mother cries
Her voice will never be heard
We do not care for our home
We turn our heads
And worry only about keeping clean our own beds.

Whatever I do and whatever I've done, has always put me on the path of the person I've never wanted to become.

J.G

Three blind mice

There were once three blind mice
And you wouldn't believe it but they were everything but nice
The first one played a lot with guns
He loved dip and would chew so much he lost his teeth and almost
all his gums
He would shoot up stores and hold up banks
He was rude and violent, he never believed in saying thanks
The second one was an even bigger mess
He loved gambling, smoking weed and preferred his women to wear
only a dress
He would sell happy pills, blue pills and dream sticks
At the end of an alley in his little red house of bricks
The third one was the worst of all
He was cold and heartless just like the months of fall
He had no interest in what the other two said
His favorite color was oddly enough, bloody red
He would snatch children right out of there bed
Something was deeply wrong inside his head
He knew what he did was a terrible crime
But what can you expect from a blind cannibal mouse with a very
disturbed and ugly mind?

Not having your true love in your life
is like being lost on a cold path
where the days are numbing,
the silence is painful
and the solitude is agonizing.

J.G

To be

I was born without instructions included

Assembled and designed for heavy usage

Ordered and shipped to this world

To be the resistance against the current

To be the shepherd against the wolves

To be a samurai with my words

And cut deep with my katana

Piercing your reality

Exposing its brink

With my bleeding pen of ink.

I will jump off the tallest temple just to be with you in the loneliest palace below the sea, where the light is absent and darkness reigns as the one true king. All because you are my mermaid, whom without, I cannot live a normal life on this Earth. I tried to capture you in my net but you caught me first in your web of love and the more I fought, the more I drowned, but you untangled me and set me free. Free to choose what is right and I will always choose you, my love.

J.G

Toward clouds

There she was
Entrapped without a cause
Chained to the TV
She begged: "lord please don't leave me!"
From head to toe
Her robe hid her glow
Her shining spirit
Muted, she could not sing a single lyric
In the darkness she was kept
Day after day, she wept
Until one day she was saved
All her chains broke away
She fled from that place
And disappeared without a trace
The image was broken
The man's true colors were spoken
And then she smiled, she found her light
God saved her, with all of his might
As her smile slowly blossomed
He said: "this is no longer your fight"
And as she said her last goodbye
Towards the clouds, she ascended into flight.

sometimes I wish I never met you.
the moment I saw you I knew I would never forget you. I
wake up thinking of your smile and fall asleep dreaming
of your body but just knowing that you are not mine
is the nightmare I have to live with every day.
you broke into my life and made everything turn
upside down, shifting my feelings all around because
the beast inside me was asleep, until you came.
now you are the only thing it actually craves.

J.G

Trenches and stitches

Imagine being able to see yourself

Different.

Every day a new mask

Every night a new moon

I shattered my mirror many years ago

And struggled picking up the pieces

Fragile parts of glass

Containing memories of a cut past

I have never been the same since then

And I will always be different

Every second itches

Because I can't forget

My skin was a battleground

Full of trenches and stitches.

I don't want to be another fish in the ocean.
I want to be the fucking Megalodon.

J.G

Urges

She wasn't always like this

Poisonous lips waiting, dying to kiss

I always told her not to stare into her own abyss

Because she wouldn't like what's inside

Even though my hands were tied

I always tried

So many times, my soul cried

I tried to stop her from using

I still remember the blood from her deep cuts, oozing

I tried to stop her from abusing

But I could never control her urge

The urge to harm herself

To gut down every pill on the shelf

The urge for auto destruction

Like a program gone bad

A program, that can no longer function.

There is no need to be ashamed of crying.
Each tear contains pain and sorrow that must be let go of
to make space for the new ones.
Hopefully, tears of joy.

J.G

Very much alive

Constant beating inside
Something very alive
Without it
I die.

There is a constant beating inside
Something dark but very much alive
Unfortunately, without it, I will fly.

There is a relentless pounding inside of me
Something very dark and sad but I know it is very much alive
And it will sentence me to death or flight.

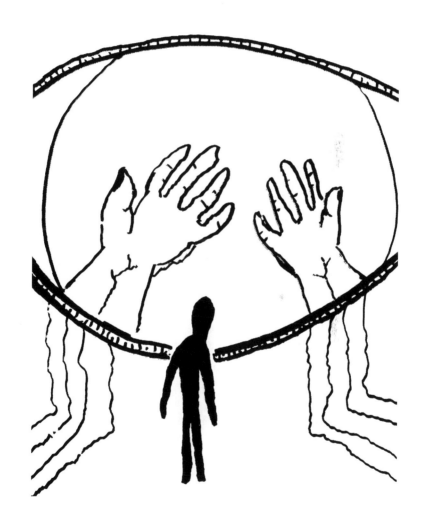

What she wants

She wants it
Every second of the day
But she doesn't show it
She wants to be on her knees
Begging for it, like a dog
She wants it, pulsating and pounding in between her legs
She wants to hug, squeeze and sink it, between her breasts
She wants to lick it
Swallow it
Taste it
She wants it so deeply
So intensely
So badly
She wants it to fill all her holes
Cover her scars
And cure her wounds
All of them
Every
Single
One.

She wants love
That's all she'll ever want.

What you did

My body just heats up!

You make me sick

I fucking hate you

I wish poison would fall gently into your cup

You hypocrite

You liar

A waste of sperm

Just a walking bag of flesh

I don't want you dead

I want you to breath painfully

Frantically

As I destroy your thoughts

And beat to soup all in your head

Because I will never forget

What you did to, inside

My once beautiful and lovely mind.

AXON:180

Some people just want to watch the world burn.
There is no deep theory or psychological analysis
That needs to be done to understand this.

J.G

When I was young

I remember my days back then, when I was young
Living free of guilt, seeking nothing but fun
Lonely I lived, with nothing but my imagination
Every day waking up was such a celebration
Now the days go by slow and troubles are all we know
But even so, maybe one day I'll play one last time in the snow

White stallion

I am the water that falls on your pain

The earth that quakes your body

The storm that floods your mind

The tide that wastes your worries

I am your strong stallion

Your only true companion

As white as God's clouds

I will take you away

Come with me, tomorrow will be a brighter day.

love is more than just a simple word.
Its roots grow deep into the mind and heart of those who
are poisoned by it. It changes their life from the way they
feel to the way they see the world around them, as if nothing
makes sense unless they are together. Time changes and so
do your thoughts. In the end, the only person that can understand
you is your other half who holds the antidote for the pain
caused by this beautiful but dangerous game of love.

J.G

Wind of fall

The chilling wind of fall

So unique it affects us all

It blows naked all the trees

And takes away the flowers from the bees

It tickles the water, makes it dance

Cutting through it like an invisible lance.

You can't swim against the current
of your inner sea forever.
The black waves of your alter ego
will wash you away
and before you drown in the depths
of your dark secrets
the sharks of your deepest fears
will tear through the delicate flesh
of self consciousness you have left.

J.G

Wolf

You will never see
How cunning the lone wolf is
With its enemy

Some people live with a storm
inside their mind
because of the clouds of doubt
hovering over them,
making the days numb and grey
while strikes of fear and guilt
hit them harder than lightning
as they find out there is no umbrella to protect them
from the inner rain of self-blame.

J.G

Young sunflower

When I saw you for the first time
I knew you were different,
like me.
Even though I knew there were many flowers in this lost field,
you stood out the most.
You and your soft leaves,
your dark eyes
and your golden smile.
You were the sunflower I chose to lay my roots near
because you are the sun that illuminates my life.

Your show

Do not settle at just being "ok"
You have been beautifully gifted
There is no shame in adding more salt and pepper to your plate
No regrets in pouring more paint upon your palette
And no embarrassment in sprinkling more water onto your leaves
Rattle like a snake and let them know where you stand
Direct your life, make it your show.

I need you in my life
I need your smile
your laughter
your smartass comments
even though I don't show it
my world is nothing without you.
I always want you around me
like the sky needs it's clouds,
I need you.

J.G

You were

You were my sun
You were my moon
You were my light
Always shining bright.

You used to hold me tight
You would never let me out of your sight
You would always protect me with all your might.

It's almost as if I was meant to suffer
To become your imprisoned poet
Your forced jester
Your sad clown,
Always able to fix your upside-down frown
As you reign, supreme leader,
With your rusty, old and broken crown.

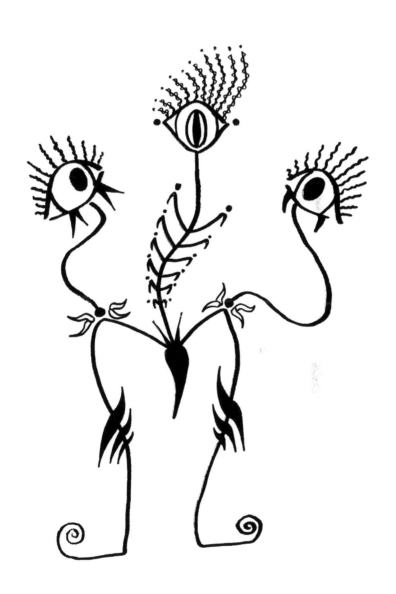

Zero three hundred hours

03:00, hard knocks on the door
Shitty Weather outside, its ready to pour
It's a struggle leaving the warmth of the cot
Too cold outside, FUCK the john, just piss in a pot
Boots on deck, gear prepped, exit the tent
Still early in the morning and I'm ready to vent
The sky is dark as the birds still sleep
Watch your step, this path is steep
Relax your mind and ease your soul
Damn, I can't wait to get home and out of this FUCKING hole.

The dark demons that live a secret life in the deepest
parts of our mind are sometimes unknown to us,
just as the many bottom dwelling creatures that live
in the forgotten parts of our immense oceans.

J.G

Zodiac

I wish you the best in this life
And the one next to come
Enjoy the stars
Forget all your scars
Never let others define you
Even though the night is pitch black
You are still part of the zodiac
Follow your own moon
And you will be
Where you need to be
Soon.

Following the path you believe in
is a rough and lonely journey
full of illusions and hostility
like wandering through a desert alone
in search for the Oasis
you see in your dreams
every single night.

J.G

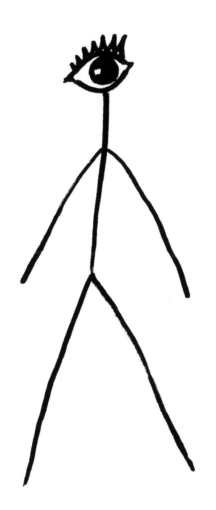

A Tarantula
slowly walks across the branch
of a dying tree.

J.G

Over the desert
Flew the last great thunder bird
King of the great sky.

J.G

As the cold crept in
The mice huddled together.
Families, survive.

J.G

One ant cannot win
but an Army, however,
is forever strong.

J.G

A small black kitten
sits, looking through a window
waiting for the moon.

J.G

The turtle sleeps, still.
basking under the proud sun
of a summer's day.

J.G

It will be the end
of humanity and life
if we do not fight.

J.G

I have seen ahead.
We walk on a path of traps,
full of snakes and thieves.

J.G

Curious and young,
they step over the shoulders
of past, fallen giants.

J.G

Like the sky will cry,
so will the people of earth
drown in heaven's tears.

J.G

You can't make happy
those who do not understand
what happiness is.

J.G

You can never see
the white owl hiding above,
in snow covered trees.

J.G

It is not the wind
that will spread the flames of evil
but the tides of men.

J.G

Listen, carefully,
to the whispers in the woods
and the cry of ghosts.

J.G

One, truly changes,
after evil stains their hands
and fear blinds their eyes.

J.G

The blood soaked the grass
after the hunter's arrow
flew through the lost prey.

J.G

In pain, she ran far.
Abandoned in the forest,
begging for answers.

J.G

Beware of the wolves,
Seek answers and ask questions
But don't graze like sheep.

J.G

You can try to fix me
but there is no glue to stick together the many
broken pieces that make me, who I truly am.
You can try to understand me but there is no instruction
manual to decipher the code of the complex algorithm
of my dark mind with which I was born.
You can try to heal me from my own toxicity
but the same poison that is deep within my veins is
the same substance that makes me feel alive.
I am the living definition of being uniquely rare.

J.G

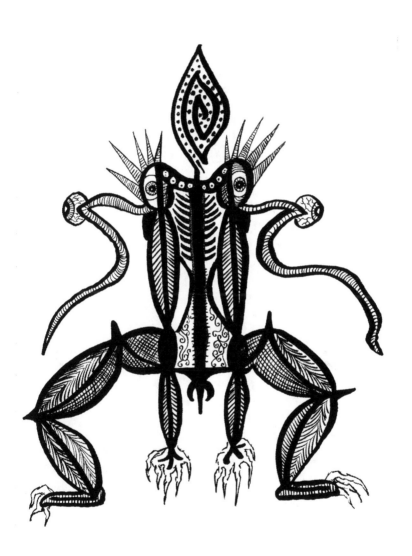

Tu eri l'unica persona con cui potevo
parlare e chiedere un consiglio.
Eri la madre che non ho mai avuto anche se mi
hai sempre trattato come se fossi tuo figlio.
Non avrei mai pensato che fosse possibile parlare con una santa
La tua risata m'illuminava la giornata
E di bonta' ne avevi sempre tanta
Ma il fatto era che eri tu a riempirmi di speranza
Anche quando mi trovavo vuoto e senza.
Mi manca il tuo cibo
Mi manca vedere il tuo sorriso
Infatti, ogni giorno senza di te e' un bivio.
E' da quando te ne sei andata che mi sento piu' freddo
E vedo tutto piu' grigio.
Non c'e' abbastanza inchiostro in questa penna con cui scrivo
Per raccontare tutte le volte in cui hai visto oro in me
Quando tutti gli altri hanno visto solo schifo.
Adesso che gli anni passano e mi trovo piu' vecchio
Vorrei poter tornare indietro per stringerti forte,
Sentire ancora una volta il tuo profumo e parlare con te per ore.
Anche se a volte non piango, sentiro' sempre questo dolore.
Fa male la mancanza di aver perso casa, madre e cuore
Perche' finche' c'eri tu, non avevo bisogno di paradiso
Ma ora che mi trovo da solo nel buio,
Rinchiuso nella prigione dentro la mia testa,
Nel mezzo del chaos di questa tempesta,
L'unica cosa che posso fare e' pregare per il tuo aiuto.
Senza di te, questo mondo non ha niente da offrire
Perche' tu eri tutto.

Dedicato a Marisa Borghesan con tanto amore e a mio
fratello e migliore amico, Andrea Borghesan.

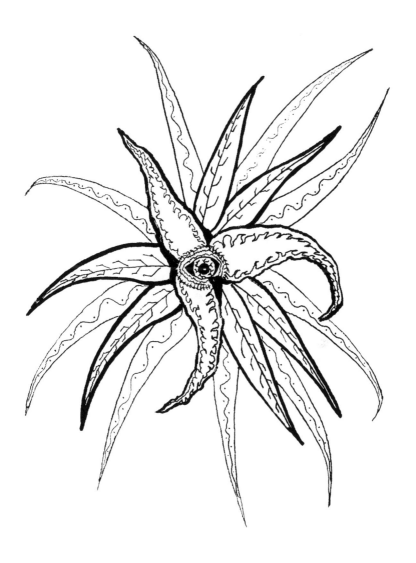

To my father, the greatest man I know whose strength, determination and willpower made him a hero forever in my eyes.

Thank You.

To Natasha:

The moon that aided me through the dark forest of my life and the lighthouse always guiding me back to shore from the raging waters of the chaotic ocean inside my ugly mind.

Thank You.

To all those who walk among us suffering silently every day because of the heavy burden of their mental conditions that they must carry.

You are not alone.

Per Virgilio e tutti gli altri.

Vi ringrazio.

The mind is a funny yet tragic thing. Few are masters of it while many are slaves to it. The human brain is a magician, capable of deceiving us, tricking us, showing us illusions, distracting us from our dreams and putting us in a puzzle where each piece becomes a riddle inside a maze of neurons and electricity as we become hypnotized and shackled by it's magic of nightmarish glory. We attend the show each day waking up to the magicians play but at which point we realize it is a conman, sometimes is too late. I believe in the power of this universe and the great hidden laws that were created from an orchestrated chaos of mystery which haunts our lives each day. A person can only take so much before they retreat into the dark solitude of their minds but some of the greatest carry a prison within them containing their previous selves locked up as we stumble across, pacing our rhythm trying to keep our demons locked even though unfortunately some times the inner gates of darkness open and it is up to us to catch it in time to avoid self destruction because we are all born without firewalls or protection of any sort to the negative programs that we are installed with. We continuously must go through trial and error to find the best version of ourselves but it is always easier said than done. I wish each story had a happy ending but sometimes our heroes become villains as we become our own worst enemies in a never ending war towards the simple pursuit of happiness. To wake up smiling, happy and proud of our new selves is the goal of so many people who cry each day and those who have no more tears to shed as well but life is both cruel and beautiful. All we can do is hope and pray for her kindness rather than her wrath.

The mental state of this nation is deteriorating rapidly more than ever. We live in dark times still hoping to see the light at the end of the tunnel but so far the question is how long will we stay blind, in darkness? Millions of people through out the world suffer from mental conditions, disorders and abnormalities. So far, none of them have ever had a voice in today's chaotic condition. Some call it natural selection while others can disagree and claim there is a vast sea of people who we either leave behind or help. No one should ever feel alone with the problems they carry. I wish the best to all people suffering in this world. No matter what, no matter where, I believe we all can try to find peace with one another but the biggest challenge is finding peace with ourselves. This book is no medicine, no cure, no antidote or miracle but I believe it was meant to somehow help. How, is up to you. Just know you are not alone friend. The battle continues and so do the tears but you WILL NEVER BE ALONE.

Poetry is and always will be a form of art but in the age we live in today, Art is under attack. Too many charlatans and mimes have seeped through the cracks of fame in order to sabotage a once well respected form of art but it's true, as people change so do times and today we need a new wave of deliverance of this art. People must understand that we live in a world of shiny lights and sparkling glitter filter effects, in fact both of those can cover up the mess we have made of the world we live in. some people might get mad and others might become believers in the imperfect beauty of dark poetry but all I can say is that I will continue to write till my fingers become stone. All we are, are bags of flesh beautifully put together but not with all the right pieces. I believe it is almost part of being human to be imperfect but once we realize this we become closer to something more than just breathing flesh. We become unique. Everyone has been given a gift, a talent or a set of skills. These are what make us amazingly different and life does everything to deviate you from your path while at the same time point you in the right direction. *Following the wind won't let you fly but it will help you feel free like the bird that does.*

Sincerely yours;

J.G

Goodbye, Friend.

The following empty pages are for you to write whatever you please. Whether it's about this book, your feelings, your dreams and your fears or simply for notes.

They're all yours.
Do as you please.